5. The

4. Correct

3. Order

2. Of

1. Biscuits

5. THE
4. CORRECT
3. ORDER
2. OF
1. BISCUITS

(and other meticulously
assembled lists of
extremely valuable nonsense)

Adam Sharp

First published in Great Britain in 2020 by Trapeze
an imprint of The Orion Publishing Group Ltd
Carmelite House, 50 Victoria Embankment
London EC4Y 0DZ

An Hachette UK Company

3 5 7 9 10 8 6 4

A CIP catalogue record for this book is
available from the British Library.

ISBN (Hardback) 978 1 3987 0172 4
ISBN (eBook) 978 1 3987 0173 1

Typeset by Born Group
Printed in Great Britain by Clays Ltd, Elcograf S.p.A

MIX
Paper from
responsible sources
FSC® C104740

www.orionbooks.co.uk

3. For my dad, who loved lists also

2. For my granddad, who raised me

1. For my mum, who was gone too soon

3. 'If people did not sometimes do silly things, nothing intelligent would ever get done'

~ *Ludwig Wittgenstein*

2. 'To appreciate nonsense requires a serious interest in life'

~ *Gelett Burgess*

1. 'List, list, O, list!'

~ *William Shakespeare*

INTRODUCTION

A list of options for the introduction

5. A lengthy anecdote about the time, while still in nappies, that I wrote my first ever list

4. An essay on why I love lists so much (which cleverly implies that I'm the world's leading listologist)

3. A look at the psychology of list-making (is my list-making compulsion related to the Oedipus complex? OCD? Could I have tendencies towards serial killing?)

2. A look at some great lists/list-makers throughout history (Moses, for example, was right into them)

1. Just get on with it

A list of New Year's resolutions

1. Make longer lists

A list of bands in order of efficacy

3. Placebo

2. The Cure

1. Prevention

A list of things it's raining . . .

8. Cats and dogs (English)

7. Old ladies and sticks (Welsh)

6. Like a pissing cow (French)

5. As from Esteri's ass (Finnish)

4. Female trolls (Norwegian)

3. Chair legs (Greek)

2. Wheelbarrows (Czech)

1. Men (hallelujah)

A list of words that sound rude but aren't

10. Fallacious

9. Kumquat

8. Penal

7. Cleat

6. Succulent

5. Titular

4. Gesticulate

3. Rectory

2. Manhole

1. Pumpkin (vegetable or incest?)

A list of English Regency slang

8. Dicked in the knob (crazy)

7. The apple dumplin' shop (breasts)

6. Lapping your congo (drinking tea)

5. The mulligrubs (feeling down)

4. Potato trap (mouth)

3. Malty (drunk)

2. Dance the blanket hornpipe (to have sex)

1. My arse on a bandbox (like hell I will)

A list of Kim Jong-Il's achievements (from his official biography)

7. Learned to walk (aged 3 weeks)

6. Learned to talk (aged 8 weeks)

5. Wrote 1,500 books and 6 full operas (at university)

4. Shot 11 holes-in-one in a golf game

3. Controlled the weather with his mind

2. Invented the hamburger

1. Never had to poop

A list of things I feared as a kid but now rarely worry about

8. Quicksand

7. Laser beams

6. The Bog of Eternal Stench

5. Daleks

4. Venus flytraps

3. Spontaneous combustion

2. *Knight Rider* getting cancelled

1. The wind changing and my face getting stuck that way*

---

* You may be thinking that's quite a short list and I was some serious badass as a child, but alas there were plenty of other things I feared, such as sharks in swimming pools, stepping on cracks in the pavement, holding on to a balloon too long and floating away with it, Miss May (scary art teacher), Venger from *Dungeons & Dragons*, a tree growing inside my stomach (from swallowing apple pips), the Bermuda Triangle, railway lines, piranhas, rabies, acid rain, moths and, finally, scarecrows, which, unlike the rest of the list, still terrify me to this day

A list of things I never worried about as a kid that terrify me as an adult

7. Parties

6. Talking to people at parties

5. Loud neighbours moving in (and having parties)

4. Dying alone

3. Making grammatical errors

2. People standing too close

1. Keanu Reeves turning out to be evil

A list of the top ten greatest animals ever

10. Animals

9. Are

8. Sentient

7. Beings

6. Not

5. Objects

4. To

3. Be

2. Ranked

1. Penguins * †

---

* Why penguins rule, part 823: In the 1990s a king penguin called Lala was rescued from a fishing net by the Nishimoto family. They built him his own air-conditioned room and he was even trained to waddle into town to collect groceries (wearing a specially made Pingu backpack)

† Why penguins rule, part 967: In 2011 a retired bricklayer, João Pereira de Souza, found a Magellanic penguin covered in oil. He nursed the penguin (who he named Dindim) back to health, and every year since Dindim has returned to visit him (because penguins are the greatest!)

A list of Victorian slang

8. Gigglemug (always smiling)

7. Bitch the pot (pour the tea)

6. Got the morbs (temporary sadness)

5. Tight as a boiled owl (drunk)

4. Poked up (embarrassed)

3. Sauce-box (the mouth)

2. Cupid's kettle drums (breasts)

1. Not up to dick (unwell)

A list of Victorian slang but with Gen Z definitions

8. Afternoonified (fleek)

7. Chuckaboo (BFF)

6. Off your chump (cray-cray)

5. Dash my wig (OMG)

4. Mutton shunter (po-po)

3. Skilamalink (sus)

2. Nanty-narking (crine/dead)

1. Shoot into the brown (taking the L)

A bonus list with the standard definition

8. Afternoonified (smartly dressed)

7. Chuckaboo (close friend)

6. Off your chump (unhinged)

5. Dash my wig (surprised)

4. Mutton shunter (police)

3. Skilamalink (suspicious)

2. Nanty-narking (having a good time)

1. Shoot into the brown (to fail)

A list of things greedy people want in different languages

7. To have their cake and eat it (English)

6. To have the moustache and drink porridge (Tamil)

5. To dance at two weddings (German)

4. To sit on two horses with one backside (Hungarian)

3. To have the butter, the money to buy the butter, and a smile from the milkmaid (French)

2. To have a cask full of wine and a drunk wife (Italian)

1. To eat a fish and sit on a dick (Russian)*

---

* And there is one more phrase – 'me want cookie and me want more cookie' – in Cookie Monsterish

A list of ideas for adverts

8. We'll drive you up the wall (stairlift installers)

7. Our business is going down the drain (plumbers)

6. Our days are numbered (calendar makers)

5. Summer special: Smoking hot body or your money back (crematorium)

4. We'll help bring out your inner child (maternity ward)

3. Our clients speak very highly of us (helium manufacturers)

2. You'll be dying to get in (cemetery)

1. We always keep it up (airline)

A list of titles for a historical thriller

7. *The Girl on the Steam Train*

6. *The Girl with the Wagon Tattoo*

5. *The Remains of the Girl*

4. *To Kill a Mockinggirl*

3. *One Hundred Years of Girlitude*

2. *Girliver's Travels*

1. *Crime and Girlishment*

A bonus list of children's books titled by commercial fiction authors

5. *Where the Wild Things' Daughters Are*

4. *The Little Prince's Daughter*

3. *The Gruffalo's Daughter*

2. *The Very Hungry Caterpillar's Daughter*

1. *The Hitchhiker's Daughter's Guide to the Galaxy*

A list of reasons to love Norway

3. In Norway *Mr Bump* from the *Mr Men* books is called *Herr Dumpidump*

2. Norwegians use the word texas to mean batshit crazy (as in '2020 has been totally texas!')

1. The Colonel-in-Chief of the Norwegian King's Guard, Brigadier Sir Nils Olav III, is a penguin

A list of *Mr Men* names in different languages

7. *Monsieur Grognon* (French *Mr Grumble*)

6. *Herr Kuddelmuddel* (German *Mr Topsy-Turvy*)

5. *Mr Tisian* (Welsh *Mr Sneeze*)

4. *Fætter Dumbum* (Danish *Mr Dizzy*)

3. *Senhor Bobo* (Portuguese *Mr Dizzy*)

2. *Gubben Glufs Glufs* (Swedish *Mr Greedy*)

1. *Don Pupas* (Spanish *Mr Bump*)

A list of the correct order of biscuits

5. Jaffa Cakes*

4. Chocolate Bourbons

3. Choco Leibniz (those fancy German ones)

2. Oreos (those fancy American ones)

1. Triple chocolate chip cookies

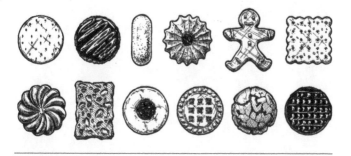

* I anticipate no little controversy about me including Jaffa Cakes on a list of biscuits because many believe them, as per their name and a tax-avoiding court case, to be cakes. I'll return to that later but for now I'll just quickly say this: you are wrong

A list of names for the baby versions of animals

7. Puffling (puffin)

6. Whelp (otter)

5. Hoglet (hedgehog)

4. Crocklet (crocodile)

3. Porcupette (porcupine)

2. Puggle (echidna)

1. Piggie Smalls (pig)

A list of animal rhymes you can use to say farewell

8. In a while, crocodile

7. Toodle-oo, kangaroo

6. Ciao for now, Jersey cow

5. Why you still here, white-tailed deer

4. Just piss off, gypsy moth

3. Go to hell, red gazelle

2. Kiss my hole, woodland vole

1. Off you fuck, crested duck

A list of films to watch if you like pasta

5. *A Fusilli Good Men*

4. *The Grand Budapesto Hotel*

3. *Lawrence of Arrabiata*

2. *Fear and Loathing in Lasagne*

1. *The Texas Chainsaw Marinara*

A list of celebrity rhymes you can use to say farewell

8. Come again soon, Reese Witherspoon

7. Have a nice day, Lana Del Rey

6. See you anon, Simon Le Bon

5. There's the door, Pauly Shore

4. Now off you feck, Gregory Peck

3. Take a hike, Dick Van Dyke

2. Fall down a well, Harvey Keitel

1. I've run out of rhymes, Beyoncé

A list of books to read if you like pasta

5. *Love in the Time of Carbonara*

4. *Pi-gnocchi-o*

3. *A Tagliatelle of Two Cities*

2. *The Heart is a Cannelloni Hunter*

1. *Remembrance of Things Pasta*

A list of things that are technically illegal in England

8. Operating a cow while drunk

7. Flying a kite in the street

6. Carrying planks of wood (in London)

5. Shaking your door mat (after 8 a.m.)

4. Singing 'Happy Birthday' (ever)

3. Sliding on ice or snow

2. Wearing a suit of armour in Parliament

1. Holding a salmon in 'suspicious circumstances'*

---

* Ridiculous as these laws may seem, they don't even come close to being as nonsensical as Jaffa Cakes being legally classified as a cake in the United Kingdom, which just shows how utterly utterly misguided our legal system can be sometimes (I studied law for almost four months at university so am clearly well qualified to make this assertion)

A list of sensible laws from around the world

5. In Arizona, it is illegal to let a donkey sleep in your bathtub

4. In Turin, local council law states you must walk your dog at least three times a day

3. In Blythe, California, you're not allowed to wear cowboy boots unless you own at least two cows

2. In Queensland, it's illegal to own a rabbit unless you're a magician

1. In Switzerland, you cannot own just one guinea pig*

---

* Guinea pigs are social animals and it's deemed cruel to deprive them of the company of other guinea pigs. Swiss law also protects parrots, goldfish, and cats from loneliness in similar ways. Why? That's just how the Swiss roll

A list of collective nouns for animals

10. A caravan of camels

9. A rhumba of rattlesnakes

8. A scurry of squirrels

7. A fluffle of rabbits

6. A waddle of penguins

5. A bouquet of pheasants

4. A pandemonium of parrots

3. A squad of squids

2. A barrel of monkeys

1. A blessing of unicorns

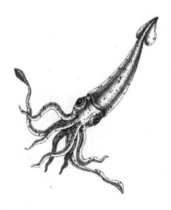

A list of the most popular names for the daughters of drummers

3. Anna One

2. Anna Two

1. Anna One Two Three Four

A list of collective nouns for people

10. A slick of lawyers

9. A coincidence?! of conspiracy theorists

8. A munity of anti-vaxxers

7. An enlargement of pianists

6. An anarchy of librarians

5. A great deal of car salesmen

4. A lot of parking attendants

3. A fuckery of prime ministers

2. A sophistication of Kardashians

1. A notherweek of builders

A list of music jokes

3. What do you call someone who hangs around with musicians?

The drummer

2. What's the difference between a drummer and a vacuum cleaner?

You have to plug one of them in before it sucks

1. What does a drummer use for contraception?

His personality*

---

* In all seriousness, I have nothing against drummers (some of my best friends are drummers)

A list of collective nouns for books

10. A pretension of literary fiction

9. A range of mountaineering guides

8. A shroud of mysteries

7. A cumulation of wealth management textbooks

6. A rash of skincare books

5. An exaggeration of autobiographies

4. A sshh-load of library books

3. A lotment of gardening books

2. A hoard of erotica

1. Too many cookbooks

A list of useful Swedish words

5. *Skitstövel* (a douchebag, literally 'shit boot')

4. *Knullruffs* (messy hair after sleeping with someone, literally 'fuck hair')

3. *Sliddersladder* (a gossip)

2. *Slutspurt* (a clearance sale, literally 'race to the end')

1. *Snuskhummer* (a pervert, literally 'filthy-minded lobster')*

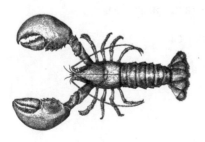

---

* Another great Swedish word was *ogooglebar* (someone, or something, that doesn't show up in an online search, literally 'ungoogleable') but sadly the Language Council of Sweden decided to drop it from its list of new words after legal pressure from Google

A list of words that are older than you think

8. Fangirl (1934)

7. OMG (1917)*

6. Legit (1897)

5. Fake news (1890)

4. Xmas (1755)

3. Hubby (1682)

2. Newfangled (1496)

1. That chonky boi is swole and thicc (217 BC)

---

* The first known use of OMG comes from a letter to Winston Churchill (in 1917). And Churchill himself later used OMG in one of his famous speeches:

> 'We shall fight on the beaches
> We shall fight on the landing grounds
> We shall fight in the fields and in the streets
> And they'll be all like omg just stop already wtf'

A list of my biggest flaws

10. Disturbingly obsessed with lists

9. Often repeat myself

7. Rubbish at counting

6. Always putting myself down

5. Terrible person

4. Often repeat myself

3. Weird toes

2. Never finish things

1.

A list of how dogs go woof woof in different languages (a ruff approximation)

8. *Voff voff* (Icelandic)

7. *Lol lol* (Tamil)

6. *Bup bup* (Catalan)

5. *Ham ham* (Albanian)

4. *Woke woke* (Burmese)

3. *Gong gong* (Malay)

2. *Wang wang* (Mandarin)

1. *Bawf* (Scots)

A list of things I believed in childhood that may have been wrong

5. Everyone gets a turn at being Prime Minister

4. Fish fingers are actual fingers

3. The A in *The A-Team* stands for Adam

2. Teachers don't exist outside of school hours

1. In the old days the whole world was black and white

A list of the sounds animals make around the world

8. *Pip pip* (Swedish mouse)

7. *Ko-ki-o* (Korean rooster)

6. *Awoo!* (Filipino lion)

5. *Nøff nøff* (Norwegian pig)

4. *I-go-go* (Russian horse)

3. *Meh* (Portuguese sheep)

2. *Gulu gulu* (Turkish turkey)

1. ???? (any fox)

A list of unnecessary, needless, and gratuitous tautologies

7. Shrugged his shoulders (what else would he shrug?)

6. Nodded her head (see above)

5. ATM machine (see also PIN number)

4. Future plans (see also past experience)

3. Fiction novel (urgh)

2. Safe haven (urghhhhhh)

1. Revert back (unforgivable)

A list of how to say 'A whole different kettle of fish' in different languages

5. These are figs from a different basket (Catalan)

4. That's another pair of sleeves (French)

3. This is flour from another sack (Spanish)

2. These are another pair of wellies (Polish)

1. This is a different dish of cabbage (Hungarian)

A list of nonsense words

10. Twaddle

9. Guff

8. Pish posh

7. Hokum

6. Mumbo jumbo

5. Baloney

4. Poppycock*

3. Claptrap

2. Codswallop

1. Jibber jabber†

---

* Some people say poppycock originates from the Dutch word for 'faeces as soft as porridge'. Others say it derives from the Dutch word for 'doll's excrement'. They're clearly talking crap
† Supposedly the term jibber jabber dates back to the 16th century but everyone knows Mr T invented it in the 1980s. I pity the fool that tries to tell him otherwise

A list of colourful exclamations

8. Great bald-faced hornets!

7. By the hokey-pokey!

6. Fuck a duck!

5. What fresh hell is this?

4. Oh, buggery botch-wagons! (strictly for posh people)

3. Blow my buttons!

2. Holy horror!

1. Jesus Christ on a raft!

A list of how people go achoo in different languages

7. *Hakushon* (Japanese)

6. *Atchim* (Portuguese)

5. *A-psik* (Polish)

4. *Hapsu* (Turkish)

3. *Tisian* (Welsh)

2. *Hatsjoe* (Dutch)

1. *Ha-ching* (Tagalog)

A list of musical artists to listen to if you like biscuits

8. Fleetwood Macaroons

7. Florentine and the Machine

6. Bourbon Jovi

5. Hob Nob Dylan

4. Jaffas on Airplane

3. Penguin Stefani

2. Oreo Speedwagon

1. Lionel Rich Tea

A list of films that sound rude but aren't

10. *Deep Impact*

9. *Inside Llewyn Davis*

8. *Fire Down Below*

7. *Octopussy*

6. *Chitty Chitty Bang Bang*

5. *Pocahontas*

4. *The Harder They Come*

3. *Silver Lode*

2. *Fists of Fury*

1. *Big*

A list of contemporary curses for your worst enemy

8. May all your snacks be really healthy

7. May your bare feet always find a Lego

6. May you forever put your USB in upside down

5. May you have more clothes than hangers

4. May all your favourite bands get into saxophone solos

3. May your boxes of Quality Street have no purple ones in it

2. May neither side of your pillow be cool

1. May your country of origin never be the first option in the drop-down box

A list of classic George W. Bush quotes (Bushisms)*

5. Families is where our nation finds hope, where wings take dream

4. I think we agree, the past is over

3. I know how hard it is for you to put food on your family

2. One of the great things about books is sometimes there are some fantastic pictures

1. Rarely is the question asked: Is our children learning?

---

* Remember when we thought he was the worst ever? LOL

A list of names things used to be called

10. Thomas Mapother, IV (Tom Cruise)

9. Joaquin Bottom (Joaquin Phoenix)

8. Johnston's Fluid Beef (Bovril)

7. Relentless (Amazon)

6. Elf-chokes (hiccups)*

5. Windfuckers (kestrels)

4. The Lunch Bunch (*The Breakfast Club*)

3. Toyz In the Hood (*Toy Story*)

2. Something That Happened (*Of Mice and Men*)

1. Snottingham (Nottingham)†

---

* Hiccups were called elf-chokes or *ælfsogoða* in Old English because it was believed that they were caused by elves (sounds plausible enough to me)
† In the Middle Ages Nottingham was known as Snotingaham ('the homestead of Snot's people') when it fell under the rule of a Saxon chief called Snot, eventually becoming Snottingham, and then, ultimately (and understandably), losing the 'S'

A list of music to listen to if you like chocolate

   7. Bay City Rolos

   6. Arctic Munchies

   5. A Daim and the Ants

   4. Picnic! At The Disco

   3. Thirty Seconds to Mars Bars

   2. Rage Against the Vending Machine

   1. Everything But The Twirl

A list of my favourite twentieth century colloquialisms

8. Tickety-boo

7. Malarkey

6. Shenanigans

5. Jiggery-pokery

4. Palaver

3. Whoops-a-daisy

2. Brouhaha

1. Gubbins

A list of names for jellyfish in different languages

7. Sea glitter (Icelandic)

6. Moon of the sea (Japanese)

5. Bride of the sea (Persian)

4. Wibbly wobbly fish (Welsh slang)

3. Seal snot (Irish)

2. Bad water (Peruvian Spanish)

1. Whale vomit (Faroese)*

---

* Honourable mention to Danish, which has several great words for jellyfish. If it's a non-stinging jellyfish it's called *vandman*, which translates to 'water man'. A stinging jellyfish is called *brandman* or 'fire man'. And then there's the general term *gople*, which derives from the Norwegian dialectical *gopla*, which essentially means 'mass of slime'.

And speaking of Norwegian, the standard word for jellyfish in Norway is *manet*, which means 'sea-nettle', a fairly evocative translation, but nothing compared to their old word *draugspy*, which means 'vomit from the ghost of a drowned person'

A list of my least favourite twentieth century colloquialisms

8. Booyah

7. Gnarly

6. Goober

5. … Not!

4. As if

3. Psych!

2. Take a chill pill

1. Party-hardy

A list of words most often spelled wrong*

7. Accomodate

6. Dilemna

5. Embarass

4. Jewelery

3. Seperate

2. Mischievious

1. Wrong

---

* Here, in case you're interested, is a poem I wrote on the subject:

EVIL MISS PELLINGS

Miss Pellings can come at any thyme
Especially when you're trying to rime

She's hear and their and everywear
With clause as sharp as grizzly bare

It's quiet likely that you'll see her
In rythm, scism, onomatopeaia

You may think she's gone, breathe a sigh of relief
But no, here she is, back to cause you more greif

– Addam Sharpe

A list of fun words beginning with the letters Fl

8. Flummery

7. Flammulation

6. Flippity-floppity-floop

5. Flimflam

4. Flobbage

3. Flibbertigibbet

2. Flamdoodle

1. Flipfloppery (not in the dictionary, but it should be)

A list of words that should be banned

10. Hols

9. Holibobs

8. Chrimbo

7. Wifey

6. Hubby (or hubster)

5. This one

4. Bants

3. Banterbus (any form of banter really)

2. Fur babies

1. Lorry (bad memories from not being able to say it as a child)

A list of reasons Bono sucks

5. Egomaniac

4. Short man complex

3. Stupid white tights

2. Always starting wars

1. Trounced at Waterloo (probably why he never takes off those sunglasses)*

---

* You may be thinking to yourself, 'Erm, Adam, I think you're confusing Bono and Napoleon Bonaparte. You do realise they're different people, right?'

To which I say, 'Okay, smart guy/girl, tell me this … have you ever seen Bono and Bonaparte in the same room?'

I rest my case

A list of whatchamacallits in different languages

7. Thingamajig (English)

6. *Chingadera* (Mexican Spanish)*

5. *Himstergims* (Danish)†

4. *Naninani* (Japanese)‡

3. *Zamazingo* (Turkish)

2. *Dingsbums* (German)

1. *Huppeldepup* (Dutch)§

---

* *Chingadera* is very much an adult version of thingamajig – it basically translates to 'the fucking thing' – so be careful using it in polite company

† In most areas of Denmark *himstergims* is spelled *himstregims*, but I went with the rarer spelling because it evokes the image of an Olympic Games, but for hamsters

‡ The Japanese word *naninani* essentially means the 'what-what'

§ The most common Dutch word for thingamajig is *dinges*. Some Dutch people do use *huppeldepup* for thingamajig, but it more often refers to an unknown person (a whatshisname). I still went with it anyway though. Because how could I not? *Huppeldepup*!

A list of things only posh people say

8. Supper

7. Vis-à-vis

6. Blotto

5. Pimms-o-clock

4. Chin chin

3. Grandmamma

2. Milieu

1. Can't chat right now, Emz, I'm literally in Cambodia

A list of fun alternatives for existing words

10. Disco chicken (peacock)

9. Food weapons (cutlery)

8. Berry fucker (blender)

7. Lego finders (feet)

6. A farm clock (rooster)

5. Food library (fridge)

4. Milk racist (lactose intolerant)

3. Domesticated rocks (bricks)

2. Prison donkey (zebra)

1. American murder log (alligator)

A list of the number of chromosomes per organism

8. Fruit fly (8)

7. Housefly (12)

6. Frog (26)

5. Fox (34)

4. Cat (38)

3. Dolphin (44)

2. Human (46)

1. Pineapple (50)*

---

* I, for one, welcome our future pineapple overlords

A list of writing tips

5. Never use a big word when a Lilliputian one will do

4. If you want your writing to be accessible and modern, avoid euphuistic and erstwhile parlance

3. Don't use obsolete words or you may jargogle your reader

2. You shouldn't clutter your prose with tautologies, pleonasms, or superfluousness

1. And never, under any circumstances, begin a sentence with AND. Or any other conjunction. Unless you want to

A list of the most satisfying words to say aloud

8. Discombobulation

7. Higgledy-piggledy

6. Zamboni

5. Nincompoop

4. Mellifluous

3. Flump

2. Kerfuffle

1. I told you so

A bonus list of the most satisfying names to say aloud

5. Kublai Khan

4. Bam Bam Bigelow

3. Evonne Goolagong

2. Boutros Boutros-Ghali

1. Engelbert Humperdinck

A list of names for book clubs

10. Page Against the Machine

9. The Plath to Enlightenment

8. Austen-tacious

7. Philip K. Dick Picks

6. Cool Story Poe

5. Painfully Shelf Aware

4. Multiple Joyce

3. It's a Hardback Life

2. We Like Big Books and We Cannot Lie

1. Prose Before Hoes

A list of the most difficult words to say aloud

8. Specificity

7. Ignominious

6. Library

5. Defibrillator

4. Worcestershire

3. Pulchritude

2. Asterisk

1. Sorry*

---

* Seems to be the hardest word

A list of how to say 'The pot calling the kettle black' in different countries

5. The owl calls the sparrow big-headed (Hungary)

4. The hospital mocks charity (France)

3. The armadillo says the turtle is too hard shelled (Venezuela)

2. The dirty one badmouths the badly washed (Brazil)

1. The eye mucus laughs at the nose dirt (Japan)

A list of anagrams

10. Elvis (lives!)

9. Halley's Comet (shall yet come)

8. Princess Diana (end is a car spin)

7. Sycophant (acts phony)

6. A Christmas Number One (means abhorrent music)

5. New Year's resolution (notions we rarely use)

4. Mother-in-law (woman Hitler)

3. Father-in-law (near halfwit)

2. Admirer (married)

1. Feeling romantic (flaming erection)

A list of the most fearsome national animals

7. Brown bear (Russia)

6. Bull (Spain)

5. Wolf (Estonia)

4. Leopard (Rwanda)

3. Black panther (Gabon)

2. Bengal tiger (India)

1. Unicorn (Scotland)

A list of things musicians in the 1990s were missing

5. Scrubs

4. Limits

3. Surprises

2. Diggity

1. Doubt

A list of great movie tag lines

7. Escape or die frying (*Chicken Run*)

6. Just deux it (*Hot Shots! Part Deux*)

5. An epic of epic epicness (*Scott Pilgrim vs. The World*)

4. The wait is ogre (*Shrek the Third*)

3. Family isn't a word. It's a sentence (*The Royal Tenenbaums*)

2. The longer you wait, the harder it gets (*The 40-Year-Old Virgin*)

1. Unwittingly, he trained a dolphin to kill the president of the United States (*The Day of the Dolphin*)

A list of ways to ensure you will be regarded as powerful and important

5. Become rich

4. Befriend celebrities

3. Win awards

2. Buy a private jet

1. Point out spelling mistakes on Twitter

A list of names for fan groups

7. Pine-nuts (Chris Pine)

6. Cumberbitches (Benedict Cumberbatch)

5. Liv Laugh Lovers (Liv Tyler)

4. McAvoyeurs (James McAvoy)

3. Degenerates (Ellen Degeneres)

2. Gould-diggers (Ellie Goulding)

1. Di-hards (Princess Diana)

A list of forgotten slang for body parts

8. Grabbing irons (fingers)

7. Daddles (hands)

6. Trillybubs (intestines)

5. Parish pickaxe (prominent nose)

4. Matrimonial peacemaker (penis)

3. Pudding-house (stomach)

2. Prayer-bones (kneecaps)

1. Cajooblies (breasts)

A list of words improved in translation

7. Comma fucker (Finnish pedant)

6. Paper vampire (Afrikaans stapler)

5. Grandpa beard (French candyfloss)

4. Hand shoe (Dutch glove)

3. Into-the-groundening (German funeral)

2. Foot finger (Portuguese toe)

1. Larynx loincloth (Hindi tie)

A list of animal names improved in translation

8. Stick pig (Danish hedgehog)

7. Sea pig (Japanese dolphin)

6. Fat goose (Icelandic penguin)

5. Dog fish (Turkish shark)

4. Threatening chicken (German turkey)*

3. Supernatural dog (Sioux horse)

2. Honey eater (Russian bear)

1. Butt troll (Norwegian tadpole)

A bonus list of translations from Mandarin

5. Public chicken (rooster)

4. Suburb wolf (coyote)

3. Cat head eagle (owl)

2. Forthright pig (porcupine)

1. Change colour dragon (chameleon)

---

* The German word is *Truthahn. Hahn* is the chicken part (a rooster, more specifically). And there's some debate whether the word *trut* is just onomatopoeic (a trut-trut-trut sound turkeys might make) or whether it actually comes from the middle German *droten* (to threaten). I'm obviously in camp *droten* because 'threatening chicken' rules

A list of classic newspaper headlines, set to the 'Roses Are Red' rhyme

5. Roses are red
Life is a journey

MAN ACCUSED OF KILLING LAWYER
RECEIVES A NEW ATTORNEY

4. Roses are red
You are for the chop

COWS LOSE THEIR JOBS AS MILK
PRICES DROP

3. Roses are red
Stick to your quarantines

CHINA MAY BE USING SEA TO HIDE
ITS SUBMARINES

2. Roses are red
Pink are hydrangeas

ONE-ARMED MAN APPLAUDS THE
KINDNESS OF STRANGERS

1. Roses are red
Wonders never cease

HOMICIDE VICTIMS RARELY TALK TO
POLICE

A list of alternative deadly sins

7. RaiSIN (just a rubbish grape)

6. MoccaSIN (snakes terrible, shoes worse)

5. Sleeping with your couSIN (very bad)

4. InSINcerity

3. SINgalongs (unless to Joy Division)

2. SINgle-use straws

1. Wearing socks with sandals

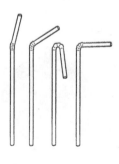

A list of my favourite types of list

5. NoveLISTS

4. IdeaLISTS

3. UnicycLISTS

2. Good LISTeners

1. Top 5s

A list of fun expressions

7. Full of beans and bus tickets

6. As rare as rocking horse shit

5. You're getting on my biscuits

4. I love you as the devil loves holy water

3. You are not a clown, you are the entire circus

2. If shoes were clues, you'd be barefoot

1. And if my grandmother had wheels she'd be a skateboard

A bonus list of Irish expressions

5. There's two gobshites in this town and he's both of them

4. The pound would squeal before he'd let go of it

3. The tide wouldn't take her out

2. If there was work in the bed, he'd sleep on the floor

1. May the cat eat you and the devil eat the cat

A list of helpful life advice

5. 'Always be sincere, even when you don't mean it.'

(Irene Peter)

4. 'Always live within your income, even if you have to borrow to do so.'

(Josh Billings)

3. 'All generalizations are bad.'

(R. H. Grenier)

2. 'We must believe in free will. We have no choice.'

(Isaac Bashevis Singer)

1. 'Always go to other people's funerals, otherwise they won't come to yours.'

(Yogi Berra)

0. 'Shoot for the moon and if you miss you will be among the stars, where there is no gravity, or oxygen, and you will just float around out there, asphyxiating and alone. Then dead.'

(Adam Sharp)

A list of expressions that are like totally whatevs

8. U ok hun

7. Let's touch base

6. Not being funny but …

5. It's been a journey

4. Sorry not sorry (Schrödinger's apology)

3. Brother from another mother

2. Sister from another mister

1. I'm a bit Marmite (yes, nauseating in large doses)*

---

* Also, people who say, 'You either love me or you hate me' (I always hate them)

A list of importmanteaus (important + portmanteaus)

7. Floordrobe (floor + wardrobe)

6. Sneezure (sneeze + seizure)

5. Shituation (shit + situation)

4. Enormouse (enormous + mouse)

3. Drunkle (drunk + uncle)

2. Zombeavers (zombie + beavers)

1. Twunt (Twitter + erm)

A list of real people born to do their jobs*

8. Les McBurney (firefighter)

7. Sara Blizzard (weather presenter)

6. Rich White (Republican)

5. Rachel B. Pullin (dentist)

4. John Bastard (Tory MP)

3. Sue Yoo (lawyer)

2. Marina Stepanova (hurdler)

1. Dick Chopp (vasectomy specialist)

---

* In 1940s and 1950s London, women were only allowed to appear nude on stage if they did not move. The senior censor who checked that such nudity rules were being upheld was called George Titman

A list of combominations (combinations + abominations)

7. Jorts (jeans + shorts)

6. Staycation (stay + vacation)

5. Chillax (chill + relax)

4. Sheeple (sheep + people)

3. Jedward (John + Edward Grimes)

2. Irregardless (irrespective + regardless)

1. Merverts (mermaids + perverts)*

---

* Something really needs to be done about those damn merverts!

A list of songs about sandwiches

5. 'Supermodel Sandwich W/Cheese' (Terence Trent D'Arby)

4. 'Purgatory Sandwich With Mustard' (Deliverance)

3. 'Sandwich of Love' (The Mentors)

2. 'Give Me Back My Sandwich' (Five Iron Frenzy)

1. 'Sandwiches Are Beautiful' (Bob King)

A list of names for the TV remote

8. The doofer

7. The jigger

6. The plink plonk

5. The turny-over-machine

4. The beep beeps

3. The hoodly-doodly

2. The blorper

1. The clickersplange

A list of club rules

5. First rule of Polite Club:

Please don't talk about Polite Club. Many thanks in advance and enjoy the rest of your day.

4. First rule of Gaslight Club:

Let's not talk about Gaslight Club. You'll only get upset again.

3. First rule of Rewrite Club:

~~Do not talk about~~ Don't discuss Rewrite Club.

2. First rule of Garrulous Club:

Do not – actually, speaking of rules, funny story, I was in the pub last week when my friend Pete walked in – do you know Pete? Funny thing about Pete, he once went on holiday to Barbados for two weeks, or was it three weeks? Hang on, it'll come to me. Actually, it was ten days …

1. First rule of Suspense Club:

A list of people killed by fruit and veg

5. Frederick III, Holy Roman Emperor (melon overdose)

4. Comic poet Antiphanes (struck by a pear)

3. Stuntman Bobby Leach (slipped on orange peel)

2. Health-food advocate Basil Brown (carrot juice poisoning)

1. Tory MP Sir William Payne-Gallwey (fell and landed on a turnip)

A list of euphemisms that really get on my you-know-whats

7. Non-traditional shopper (looter)

6. Alternative dentation (false teeth)

5. Netflix expert (unemployed)

4. Health alteration specialist (assassin)

3. Bad luck when it comes to thinking (stupid)

2. Fast driving award (speeding ticket)

1. Living impaired (dead)

A bonus list of euphemisms about dying from around the world

5. Put aside your clogs (Denmark)

4. Throw out your best skates (Russia)

3. Hang your tennis shoes (Mexico)

2. Go to the land of no hats (Haiti)

1. Go take your free kick at Hitler's backside (my granddad's house)

A list of my dream jobs

8. Water slide tester

7. Professional cuddler

6. Private island caretaker

5. Panda nanny

4. Minding my own business

3. Releaser of the hounds

2. Crusher of enemies

1. Head of Potatoes

A list of reasons to love Finland

5. When you finish your Finnish PhD you get a top hat and a sword

4. There's a library in Helsinki that has a sauna

3. Mobile phone throwing is a national sport

2. There's an annual day for celebrating failure

1. The Finnish word *Juoksentelisinkohan* means 'I wonder if I should run around aimlessly?'

A list of festive celebrities

7. Christmas Eve Saint Laurent

6. Elf Macpherson

5. Michael Candy Caine

4. Oprah Wintery

3. Angelina Jolly

2. Wreath Witherspoon

1. Kim Kardashian-Through-The-Snow

A list of unusual fears

8. Lutraphobia (otters)

7. Nomophobia (no mobile reception)

6. Gowiththeflowbia (easygoingness)

5. Hippopotomonstrosesquipedaliophobia
(long words)

4. Aibohphobia (palindromes)

3. Ragmanaphobia (anagrams)

2. Baracknophobia (Obama)

1. Twitophobia (reaching character limit bef

A list of how to say 'Beating around the bush' in different languages

5. Circling the almond (Maltese)

4. Getting the partridge dizzy (Spanish)

3. Doing the egg dance (German)

2. Giving birth to a calf (Russian)

1. Prancing like a cat around hot porridge (Finnish)

A list of alternatives to 'When pigs fly' in different countries*

7. When donkeys fly (Italy)

6. When tractors will fall (Slovakia)

5. When monkeys fly out of my butt (Canada)+

4. When hens have teeth (France)

3. When the pig in yellow slippers climbs the pear tree (Bulgaria)

2. When cats grow horns (Indonesia)

1. When the 7–Eleven closes (Thailand)

---

* My absolute favourite is, 'That'll happen when the garden is full of ducks, holding pastry in their hands,' from a book claiming it to be Turkish. However, I asked many Turkish speakers and not one had ever heard of it (which is why it sadly didn't make the list). With sayings like this there are often many variants from each country and I'm not interested in listing the most common or up-to-date. In fact, my favourites are usually the obscure ones, known only to specific generations or regions. But nevertheless I do always insist on finding at least two native speakers who know the phrase before including it
+ The Canadian phrase is more specifically from *Wayne's World*, starring Canadian comedian Mike Myers

A list of classic malaphors*

8. Love is a dish best served cold

7. It's not rocket surgery

6. We'll burn that bridge when we get to it

5. People in glass houses shouldn't dance like nobody's watching

4. Desperate times come to those who wait

3. If you want something done right, you're part of the problem

2. Money doesn't fall far from the tree

1. Whatever doesn't kill you will try, try again

A bonus list of classic malapropisms†

5. Stop looking for escape goat

4. You're always going off on a tandem

3. Patience is a virgin

2. You're a wolf in cheap clothing

1. I deserve proper constipation for my work

---

* A malaphor is when two figures of speech (idioms, clichés, aphorisms etc.) get mixed together
† A malapropism is when one word in a figure of speech is mistaken for another, similar sounding word

A list of alternatives to the name Benedict Cumberbatch

7. Buckminster Chowderpants

6. Bentobox Crumplehorn

5. Bumpersticker Cogglesnatch

4. Bongobopper Toodlesnoot

3. Tumbledaddy Gibbygobbler

2. Thunderbeaver Skuzzledink

1. Billyray Snickersbar

A list of the worst trends in history

8. Fidget spinners

7. Planking

6. Magic Eye pictures (because I could never do them)

5. Candy Crush (because of the 8 million daily invites)

4. Keep Calm memes

3. Flowers in beards

2. Man buns

1. Burning witches

A bonus list of the best trends in history

5. *Snake* on Nokia

4. Push Pops

3. Garbage Pail Kids

2. Myspace

1. Books of lists

A list of historical figures and their feelings towards cats

7. Abraham Lincoln (lover)

6. Mussolini (hater)

5. Anne Frank (lover)

4. Genghis Khan (hater)

3. Florence Nightingale (lover)

2. Ivan the Terrible (hater)

1. Erwin Schrödinger (undecided)

A list of middle names

8. Delight (Quincy Jones)

7. Hercules (Elton John)

6. Shrader (Jennifer Lawrence)

5. John Mungo (Hugh Grant)

4. Bass (Courteney Cox)

3. Gerard (Mike Tyson)

2. Tiffany (Richard Gere)

1. Macauley Culkin (Macauley Culkin)*

---

* Macauley Culkin's original middle name is Carson but he asked his fans on Twitter what he should change it to and promised to legally adopt whatever they chose. They decided he should be called Macauley Macauley Culkin Culkin, which actually shows quite a lot of restraint. I, for example, would have gone with one of these:

5. Macauley Sulkin Culkin

4. Macauley Loves-Giblets Culkin

3. Macauley Forever-Home-Alone Culkin

2. Macauley Wets-The-Bed Culkin

1. Macauley This-Is-A-Desperate-Cry-For-Help Culkin

A list of bonus middle name facts

3. You may think Michael J. Fox's middle name begins with a J, but actually he just went with that letter because it sounds cool (his middle name is in fact Andrew)

2. The reason T. S. Eliot insisted that his middle initial always be used was because he was all too aware of what T. Eliot spelled backwards

1. My middle initial is C, which is THE only thing about my extremely embarrassing middle name I'll ever reveal. So there!

A list of strange things that have sold on eBay

7. Unwanted Brussels sprouts

6. An air guitar (autographed)

5. A town in California

4. James Blunt's sister (she ended up marrying the man who won)

3. A ghost in a jar

2. The meaning of life

1. A suit of armour for a guinea pig

A list of the most predictable endings ever

5. *The Passion of the Christ* (spoiler: Jesus dies)

4. *Titanic* (spoiler: it sinks)

3. Every romcom (spoiler: they get together)

2. *Shutter Island* (spoiler: it's stupid)

1. The song 'Ten Green Bottles' (spoiler: no more left standing on the wall)

A bonus list of film titles that gave away their endings

5. *Saving Private Ryan*

4. *Death of a Salesman*

3. *Free Willy*

2. *Lone Survivor*

1. *The Assassination of Jesse James by the Coward Robert Ford*

A list of famous books with fruit in the title

8. *A Clockwork Orange*

7. *The House on Mango Street*

6. *The Grapes of Wrath*

5. *War and Peach*

4. *Lime and Plumishment*

3. *The Girl with the Dragon Fruit Tattoo*

2. *The Berry Hungry Caterpillar*

1. *The Chronicles of Banania*

A list of how to say 'All talk and no action' around the world

5. All hat and no cattle (Texas)

4. All noise and few walnuts (Spain)*

3. A lot of foam and not much chocolate (Dominican Republic)

2. The thunder is loud, but the rain is light (China)

1. If he made 100 knives, none would have a handle (Iran)

---

* *Mucho Ruido y Pocas Nueces (All Noise and Few Walnuts)* is also the Spanish title of Shakespeare's *Much Ado About Nothing*

A list of celebrities who are either dog people or cat people

8. Woofy Allen (dog person)

7. David Meowie (cat person)

6. Bark Obama (dog)

5. Kitty Purry (cat)

4. LL Drool J (dog)

3. Catalie Portman (cat)

2. Spaniel Radcliffe (dog)

1. Fleas Witherspoon (both)

A list of my favourite international idioms

7. Like a crocodile in a wallet factory (Puerto Rican Spanish for nervous)

6. Not my circus, not my monkeys (Polish for not my problem)

5. You're scratching a lion's balls with a short stick (Afrikaans for pushing your luck)

4. He slid in on a shrimp sandwich (Swedish for being privileged)

3. Drag me backwards into a birdhouse (Norwegian for surprised)

2. Life is not a pony farm (German for life is hard)

1. You work less than Tarzan's tailor (Spanish for lazy)

A list of my thoughts about 'liking' a post on social media

3. Boring

2. Weak

1. Everyone does it

A list of why replying with 'this pleases me' is better

3. Enigmatic

2. Suggests people should curry your favour

1. It's what Benedict Cumberbatch would do

A list of the phrase 'It's all Greek to me' in different languages

7. This is a Spanish village to me (Czech)

6. This is a Czech movie (Polish)

5. This is a town in Russia (Danish)

4. It looks like fried calabash fritters (Burmese)

3. Is this ghost script? (Cantonese)

2. I can't make any chocolate from that (Dutch)

1. I only understand 'train station' (German)

A list of words Shakespeare invented

8. Braggartism

7. Hobnob

6. Bedazzled

5. Pedantical

4. Skimble-skamble

3. Swagger

2. New-fangled

1. Plumpy

A bonus list of Shakespearean insults

5. Thine face is not worth sunburning

4. Your brain is as dry as the remainder biscuit after voyage

3. Away, you three-inch fool!

2. You, minion, are too saucy

1. I do desire that we may be better strangers

A list of what syphilis was originally called in different countries

7. The Italian Disease (France)

6. The French Disease (Italy)

5. The British Disease (Tahiti)

4. The Polish Disease (Russia)

3. The German Disease (Poland)

2. The Spanish Disease (the Netherlands)

1. The Chinese Pox (Japan)

A list of rude bird names

8. Willie Wagtail

7. Fluffy-backed Tit-babbler

6. Dickcissel

5. Pygmy Nuthatch

4. Horned Screamer

3. Masked Booby

2. Common Shag

1. Stormcock

A list of words recently added to the *Oxford English Dictionary*

7. Sprogged (to have kids)

6. Begrudgery (envy)

5. Cock-a-doodle-doing (boastful)

4. Angeliferous (magnificent)

3. Schmancy (excessively fancy)

2. Bawbag (scrotum)

1. Jerkface (an obnoxious person)

A list of the best puppets, in order

5. Zippy

4. Oscar the Grouch

3. Kermit and Miss Piggy (can't separate them)*

2. Gordon the Gopher

1. Cookie Monster (obviously)

A bonus list of the wisdom and eloquence of Cookie Monster

3. 'Count your cookies, not your problems'

2. 'No cry because cookie is finished. Smile because cookie happened'

1. 'Om nom nom nom'

---

*Miss Piggy voice: 'Suits me just fine!'

A list of drinking noises in different languages

7. Glug glug glug (English)

6. *Klok klok klok* (Dutch)

5. *Gu-dong gu-dong* (Mandarin)

4. *Bakbuk bakbuk* (Hebrew)

3. *Goku goku* (Japanese)

2. *Schlürf* (German)

1. Aaaahhhhhhhhh (Universal Language of
the Grandfather)

A list of useful old words

8. Poop-noddy (a fool)

7. Fribbler (a commitment-phobe)

6. Gongoozle (to stare at a canal)

5. Beazled (exhausted)

4. All-overish (unwell everywhere)

3. Vampirarchy (like the patriarchy, but with vampires)

2. Gong-hole (toilet)

1. Unbepissed (not yet soaked with urine)

A list of the sounds made by Rice Krispies in different languages

7. Snap! Crackle! Pop! (English)

6. *Knap! Knaetter! Knak!* (Afrikaans)

5. *Riks! Raks! Poks!* (Finnish)

4. *Pim! Pum! Pam!* (Mexican Spanish)

3. *Cric! Crac! Croc!* (Canadian French)

2. *Piff! Paff! Puff!* (Swedish)

1. *Knisper! Knasper! Knusper!* (German)

A list of things you rarely see these days

8. A kit without a caboodle

7. Rack without ruin

6. Dribs without drabs

5. Bits without bobs

4. Vim without vigour

3. Thoughts without prayers

2. Bono without sunglasses

1. Wither without you (ohhhh-ohhhh)*

---

* You try to appear like you have cool taste in music but then you make a U2 reference and give yourself away, and you give, and you give, yeah you give yourself away

A multitudinous agglomeration of pantagruelian words that beguile with their splendiferousness

7. Boondoggle

6. Braggadocio

5. Slangwhanger*

4. Knickknackatory

3. Spaghettification

2. Adventuresomeness

1. Hemidemisemiquaver (should be said aloud and fast)

---

* Slangwhanger (a loud abusive speaker or offensive writer) goes particularly well with another favourite of mine, slubberdegullion (a worthless wretch).

For example … 'Donald Trump is a slangwhanging slubberdegullion and I'm sick and tired of his skulduggery'

A list of reasons why dolphins are total badasses

5. They chew on toxic puffer fish to get high

4. They can kill sharks with their noses

3. They love admiring themselves in mirrors

2. They enjoy orgies and go on killing sprees when sexually frustrated

1. They refuse to stand for national anthems*

---

* Dolphins are also incredibly intelligent. So intelligent that within a week of being in captivity they can train people to stand on the very edge of the pool and throw them fish

A list of the loudness of things in decibels

8. Refrigerator hum (40)

7. Hoover (70)

6. Motorbike (90)

5. Police siren (120)

4. Plane taking off (140)

3. Shotgun blast (160)

2. Saturn V rocket launch (210)

1. Someone eating popcorn during a film (5,000)

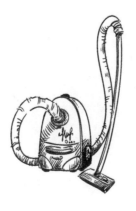

A list of international terms for the practice of each person covering their own expenses at a restaurant

5. Going Dutch (England)

4. English style (Egypt)

3. American style (Mexico)

2. Pay the bill the German way (Turkey)

1. By the law of Christ, each one with his own stew (Guatemala)

A list of types of exercise I try to avoid

7. Running my mouth

6. Jumping to conclusions

5. Pushing my luck

4. Kicking up a fuss

3. Skating on thin ice

2. Dancing with death

1. Swimming with the fishes

A list of types of drunk according to scientists[*]

5. The Hemingway (personality does not change)

4. The Mary Poppins (becomes much happier)

3. The Nutty Professor (becomes more social)

2. The Mr Hyde (becomes more hostile)

1. The Trump (becomes completely incoherent)[†]

---

[*] Interesting fact about drunkenness – in ancient Persia all important debates took place with everyone drunk and then again with everyone sober, or vice versa, because an idea wasn't considered credible unless it sounded good in both states

[†] I should mention that I made the last one up (and I'm no scientist)

A list of things a person drinks like ...

7. A fish (English)

6. A pelican (Hungarian)

5. A cow (Austrian German)

4. A dragon (Polish)

3. A shoemaker (Russian)

2. A hole (French)

1. A rainbow (Czech)

A list of spoonerisms

5. Cop porn (popcorn)

4. Don't pet the sweaty things (don't sweat the petty things)

3. Bully fooked (fully booked)

2. Bad salad (sad ballad)

1. Lack of pies (pack of lies)*

---

* I had another good one but such is my hatred of top 6s that I decided I'd rather a five listing (live fisting).

In case you were wondering about the other good one, it was the name of a furniture showroom in New Zealand – Shack of Sit

A list of international names for the @ symbol

8. Alpha twirl (Norwegian)

7. Strudel (Hebrew)

6. Cinnamon roll (Swedish)

5. Little duck (Greek)

4. Monkey bracket (German)

3. Meow sign (Finnish)

2. Moon's ear (Kazakh)

1. The 'at' symbol (English, the language of Shakespeare)

A bonus list of old English words for the exclamation mark (to show the English language can be inventive when it wants to be!)

5. Shriek-mark!

4. Wham!

3. Screech!

2. Dog's dick!

1. Shout-pole!

A list of alluring alliterations

7. Power to the people

6. Being b-b-b-b–bad to the bone

5. *Backstreet's Back* by Backstreet Boys

4. Father figure (as replacement for dad bod)

3. Whispering words of wisdom

2. Jibber jabbering

1. Doing dastardly deeds

A list of proposed new meanings for existing words

10. Minimum (a tiny mother)

9. Out of bounds (an exhausted kangaroo)

8. Knickers (people that steal things)

7. Lobsters (people that throw things)

6. Kidnapping (a sleeping child)

5. Whisky (a bit like a whisk)

4. Willy-nilly (impotent)

3. Avoidable (what a matador tries to do)

2. Heroes (what a guy in a boat does)

1. Cowards (in the direction of a cow)

A separate list because this is so good it deserves its own one

1. The word flattery should mean a flat battery in a car (because it gets you nowhere)

A list of proposed PETA-friendly idioms

8. Don't be so fig-headed

7. Like a broth to a flame

6. Sent on a wild juice chase

5. A leotard can't change its spots

4. Like a yam to the slaughter

3. Not enough room to swing a cactus

2. The world is your toaster

1. Hung like a horseradish

A list of how to say 'A few sandwiches short of a picnic' in different countries

5. She has mambo in the head (Argentina)

4. It's splashing on his lighthouse (Czechia)

3. The kangaroos are loose on the top paddock (Australia)

2. He doesn't have all the Moomins in the valley (Finland)

1. The wheel is spinning but the hamster is dead (Sweden)

A bonus list of English variants of 'A few sandwiches short of a picnic'

3. A few fish short of a hat stand

2. A few tacos short of a combo plate

1. A few penguins short of a lawnmower

A list of the worst types of list

8. Shopping lists (lead to shopping)

7. To-do lists (lead to having to do things)

6. Clickbait lists (number 1 will blow your mind!!!)

5. Colonialists (bad)

4. Top 4 lists (evil)

3. Longlists (too long)

2. Shortlists (too short)

1. Santa lists (too many clauses)

A list of names for ladybirds around the world

7. Voodoo bug (Korea)

6. Little shoemaker (Iran)

5. Bishy barnabee (Norfolk)

4. Crawl Paul (Burgenland)

3. Stinky little turtle (China)*

2. Reddish female thing (Basque Country)†

1. Stubby red cow (Wales)

---

* 'Stinky little turtle' isn't the general term for a ladybird but rather describes a specific type of ladybird (one that omits a strange smell) found in certain parts of China. The standard name for a ladybird in Mandarin translates to 'ladle bug'
† This is an etymological translation for the common word for ladybird in Basque – *marigorringo* – where *mari* originally meant 'something female', and *gorringo* meant 'reddish colour'. They are also sometimes called *amona mantangorri* which today would be understood to mean 'red apron granny'

A bonus list of brilliantly matter-of-fact Welsh translations

5. Earth pig (badger)

4. Woolly plum (peach)

3. Big mouse (rat)

2. Smelly dog (skunk)

1. Fat cheeks (hamster)

A list of Victorian illness names

8. The collywobbles (upset tummy)

7. A queer cog (rotten tooth)

6. The horrors (depression)

5. Dropsy (oedema)

4. Strangery (rupture)

3. A churchyard cough (one likely to be fatal)

2. Scrivener's palsy (writer's cramp)

1. The unpleasantness (nothing good)

A list of phrases to be used in conjunction with Joe Biden's 'Lying dog-faced pony soldier'

5. Go kiss a jellyfish, ya mutton-munchin' mime grabber

4. Laugh it up, ya Twizzler-chompin cake walker

3. You're hitch-hikin' to Memphis without a bindle, ya tomato-stewed gindaloon

2. Take a ruby red look at this ninny-lovin' cobra man

1. Cram it in your nethers, ya jazz-jivin' gopher gobbler

A list of countries with the number of heavy metal bands per 1 million people

7. China (0.1)

6. Jamaica (0.3)

5. Thailand (2)

4. Cuba (6.4)

3. Japan (11)

2. Russia (14)

1. Finland (532)

A list of the number of people killed annually by ...

8. Roller coasters (4)

7. Sharks (6)

6. Vending machines (8)

5. Champagne corks (24)

4. Cows (37)

3. Hot dogs (77)

2. Pen lids (115)

1. Exaggerated statistics (2.7 billion)

A list of meanings of country names

7. Island of Rabbits (Spain)

6. Navel of the Moon (Mexico)

5. I Go to the Beach (Nauru)

4. Hippopotamus (Mali)

3. Land of the Frizzy-Haired People (Papua New Guinea)

2. Land of the Thunder Dragon (Bhutan)

1. There (Brunei)

A list of how to tell someone to get lost in different countries

8. Go fry some asparagus (Colombia)

7. Go ski into a spruce (Finland)

6. Go collect some ants (Hungary)

5. Go to the farm to catch butterflies (Russia)

4. Go mushrooming (Latvia)*

3. Go get fucked by a blind bear (Albania)

2. Go stick a boat up your ass with the oars out (Italy)

1. I said good day, sir (England)

---

* Easily the most savage insult of them all seeing as mushrooms are the worst thing on the face of planet earth

A list of bartender jokes

3. Comic Sans and Times New Roman walk into a bar.

'Get out!' shouts the bartender. 'We don't serve your type in here.'

2. E Flat and G walk into a bar.

'Get out!' shouts the bartender. 'We don't serve minors in here.'

1. 'Get out!' shouts the bartender. 'We don't serve your kind in here.'

A time traveller walks into a bar.

A list of what Laurel and Hardy are called in different languages

5. *Flip i Flap* (Polish)

4. *Stanlio e Ollio* (Italian)

3. *Gøg og Gokke* (Danish)

2. *Helan och Halvan* (Swedish)

1. *Dick und Doof* (German)*

---

* You may be wondering if these names have any particular meaning. The Polish version is simply fun to say aloud (Flip and Flap!). *Stanlio e Ollio* is an Italian rendering of their first names (Stan and Oliver). *Helan och Halvan* translates to The Whole and The Half. *Dick und Doof* translates to Fat and Daft. And *Gøg og Gokke* basically means Cuckoo and Bonk. Cuckoo is probably a reference to Laurel and Hardy's theme song, 'The Dance of the Cuckoos', while the bonk part probably comes from Hardy's fondness for bonking Laurel over the head

A list of alternatives to 'Say cheese!' when taking someone's picture

8. Kimchi! (South Korea)

7. Omelette! (Sweden)

6. Cabbage! (Bulgaria)

5. Pea soup! (Estonia)

4. Ant shit! (Germany)

3. Pineapples can't pee! (Brazil)

2. Pepsi! (Thailand)

1. Smile, please (Poland)

A list of descriptions that have actually appeared in tabloid newspapers[*]

7. Stool-powered man-band (Westlife)

6. Step-climbing meat-puncher (Rocky)

5. Revered reptile (tortoise)

4. Highly-regarded breakfast drink (orange juice)

3. Tiny totalitarian (Kim Jong-Il)

2. Psychotic airborne scumbags (seagulls)

1. Entitled pork chop (Peppa Pig)

---

[*] These are sometimes referred to as knobbly monsters – a descriptive phrase (often contrived) used to avoid repeating the name of a person, place, or object in an article

A list of the phrase 'A leopard can't change its spots' in different countries

5. Dog will not become bacon (Hungary)

4. Those born round can't die square (Italy)

3. A dog cannot get out of the habit of eating shit (China)

2. Only the grave will cure the hunchback (Russia)

1. Death is the only remedy for stupidity (Japan)

A list of things that are unlucky around the world

8. Friday the 17th (Italy)

7. Tuesday the 13th (Greece)

6. Keys on a table (Sweden)

5. Upside down bread (France)

4. Green hats (China)

3. Yellow flowers (Russia)

2. Whistling indoors (Lithuania)

1. Skydiving without a parachute (all countries)

A list of famous book titles with added clickbait

5. *You Simply Won't Believe How Many Flew Over the Cuckoo's Nest*

4. *Fifty Mind-blowing Shades of Grey (No. 7 is EPIC)*

3. *You'll Flip When You See What Madame Bovary Looks Like Now*

2. *Every Single Year of Solitude, Definitively Ranked*

1. *Nobody Can Figure Out Where Wally Is, And It's Driving Them CRAZY*

A list of German words that begin with K

7. *Krimskrams* (knick-knacks)

6. *Krawattenmuffel* (one who doesn't like wearing ties)

5. *Kummerspeck* (weight gained from comfort eating, literally 'grief bacon')

4. *Kindergarten* (nursery school, literally 'children garden')*

3. *Kümmerling* (wimp)

2. *Krankenwagen* (ambulance, literally 'sick person car')

1. *Kaputt* (broken)

---

* Here's a poem I wrote that includes the word Kinder:

ROUGH? PLOUGH THROUGH THOUGH

They say if wordplay makes you numb
Math puns make you number

And if you stretch out every limb
It will surely get you limber

But though your children may be kind
The German kids are Kinder

And eye rhymes can be wild
But these ones just bewilder

A list of misnomers

8. Cat burglar (not a cat)

7. Guinea pig (not a pig)

6. Funny bone (not a bone, not funny)

5. White chocolate (not chocolate)

4. Baby food (no babies in it)

3. Lone Ranger (always with his sidekick)

2. The Neverending Story (ends)

1. Jaffa Cakes (NOT A CAKE!)

A bonus list of cakes that are also in no way a proper cake

3. Potato cake

2. Cheesecake

1. Urinal cake

A list of ways to start a conversation with a cat in different countries

7. Pss-pss-pss (England)

6. *Kiss-kiss-kiss* (Finland)

5. *Pish-pish-pish* (Iran)

4. *Mee-mee-mee* (Myanmar)

3. *Minou-minou-minou* (France)

2. *Ming-ming-ming* (Philippines)

1. What's new pussycat, whoa, oh whoa (Wales)

A list of my thoughts on beginning correspondence with 'Dear Sirs or Madams'

3. Dull

2. Binary

1. What is this, the 1800s?

A list of why beginning correspondence with 'Dear Gentlebeings' is better

3. Pizzazzy

2. Inclusive

1. Hints that you may be a superior (but friendly) alien life form

A list of previous names of musical artists

8. Shrinky Dinks (Sugar Ray)

7. The Sellouts (Nirvana)

6. The Sex Maggots (Goo Goo Dolls)

5. Steveland Judkins (Stevie Wonder)

4. Johnny and the Moondogs (The Beatles)

3. Shrug (Snow Patrol)

2. Hollycaust (Frankie Goes to Hollywood)

1. In Praise of Lemmings (Culture Club)

A list of things that can't be done simultaneously

7. Pinch your nose and say 'hmm' for more than three seconds

6. Breathe and swallow

5. Hum and whistle

4. Have your cake and eat it

3. Watch *Forrest Gump* and not cry

2. Be in China and check Facebook

1. Be productive and have a Twitter*

---

* Please forgive the many Twitter references, but this book would never have happened without it. I've always been a Luddite and barely used any social media until late 2018, when I decided to have a go at tweeting. The character limits had just been increased from 140 to 280 and this meant that, as long as I kept them short, I could fit a list into a single tweet. Somehow these became popular, and it has been a great source of joy to me that a solitary lifelong obsession has been so warmly received by the wonderful and witty people that follow me (and who regularly contribute improvements for existing lists and ideas for new ones)

A list of great puns

10. I was up all night trying to think of the perfect pun. And then it dawned on me

9. In America, when you've seen one shopping centre, you've seen a mall

8. It's hard to explain puns to kleptomaniacs because they always take things literally

7. It's also hard for people to take pictures of themselves in the shower because they often have selfie steam issues

6. I once saw an innuendo competition advertised in the paper. So I entered my wife

5. What's the difference between a well-dressed man and an exhausted dog? One wears a suit, the other just pants

4. I bought a blacksmith's dog last week. As soon as I got him home he made a bolt for the door

3. Why do teenagers travel in groups of three or five? Because they can't even

2. I still remember the day I realised my girlfriend was a keeper. She had massive gloves on

1. What happened to the cocky lion tamer? He was consumed by his own pride

A list of the time taken to reach 50 million users

8. *Pokémon Go* (19 days)

7. Twitter (2 years)

6. Facebook (3 years – suck it, Facebook)

5. TV (13 years)

4. Radio (38 years)

3. Telephone (50 years)

2. Cars (62 years)

1. Soap and water in male toilets (any day now)

A list of useful Cockney rhyming slang

7. Pete Tong (wrong)

6. Barney Rubble (trouble)

5. Bob Hope (soap)

4. Miley Cyrus (coronavirus)

3. Charlie Sheen (quarantine)

2. Donald Trump (elbow bump)

1. Cheryl Cole (toilet roll)

A list of foods and the percentage of people that hate them

8. Coriander (11)

7. Raisins (17)

6. Mushrooms (18)

5. Brussels sprouts (21)

4. Marmite (33)

3. Olives (38)

2. Liver (43)

1. White chocolate (should be 100 because it's a crime against humanity)

A list of international Smurf names

5. *Grande Puffo* (Italian Papa Smurf)

4. *Tarzan Schlumpf* (German Wild Smurf)

3. *Smurf Robusto* (Portuguese Hefty Smurf)

2. *Dulifuli* (Hungarian Grouchy Smurf)

1. *Kluk Fuk* (Czech Scruple the villain)

A list of Tom Swifties*

8. 'My surgery went okay,' Tom said, half-heartedly

7. 'I don't know what these shoes are laced with,' Tom said, tripping

6. 'Be quiet while I water down this orange juice,' Tom said, concentrating

5. 'You'll love my impression of a Siberian dog,' Tom said, in a husky voice

4. 'I've dropped the toothpaste,' Tom said, crestfallen

3. 'I've fallen over in the dog park,' Tom said, shitfaced

2. 'Why must everything be put in numbered order,' Tom said, listlessly

1. 'I know how COVID-19 began,' Tom said, right off the bat

---

* Tom Swifties are a type of punning using adverbs or adverbial phrases in dialogue attributions

A list of Croakers[*]

5. 'Clare, I'm splitting up with you,' Tom declared

4. 'I deserve this makeover,' Tom explained

3. 'I suppose I should put some clothes on,' Tom panted

2. 'I'm not quite the first person to arrive at your party, am I?' Tom second-guessed

1. 'And then they built me a prosthetic penis,' Tom remembered

---

[*] Croakers are similar to Tom Swifties but the pun in the dialogue attribution is a verb rather than an adverb

A list of existing titles for celebrity memoirs[*]

7. *Pryor Convictions* (Richard Pryor)

6. *Trowel and Error* (Alan Titchmarsh)

5. *Sein Language* (Jerry Seinfeld)

4. *Kiss and Make-Up* (Gene Simmons)

3. *Out of Synch* (Lance Bass)

2. *Don't Hassel the Hoff* (David Hasselhoff)

1. *Cybill Disobedience* (Cybill Shepherd)

A bonus list of title ideas for future celebrity memoirs

7. *Lohan Behold* (Lindsay Lohan)

6. *Biden: My Time* (Joe Biden)

5. *I'll Grant Hugh That* (Hugh Grant)

4. *Acts of Barbarity* (Barbara Windsor)

3. *Brydon Prejudice* (Rob Brydon)

2. *As I Liv and Breathe* (Liv Tyler)

1. *Hanks for Everything* (Tom Hanks)

---

[*] Honourable mention for the memoir of Vic Reeves, real name Jim Moir, which is called *Me: Moir*

A list of expressions for simultaneous sun and rain

5. Foxes are taking a bath (Finland)

4. A poor man got rich (Kazakhstan)

3. Witches are combing their hair (Catalonia)

2. The devil is making pancakes (Oldenburg)

1. A zombie is beating his wife for salty food (Haiti)

A list of the names for bats (the flying things, not the wooden sticks) in different languages

5. Butterfly of the night (Maltese)

4. Little evening one (Italian)

3. Little fool (Irish)

2. Not a ghoul (Polish)

1. Flutter mouse (German)*

---

* Much was made of the foolishness of consuming bats in the wake of COVID-19, but consuming their spit could actually be beneficial. The saliva from the *Desmodus rotundus* (vampire bat) is an anticoagulant and it's being developed into a medicine (with the snazzy name Draculin)

A list of excellent real business names

7. Lawn Order (landscape gardeners)

6. Vinyl Resting Place (record store)

5. You Should Be Shot (portrait photographer)

4. Hairy Pop-Ins (pet groomers)

3. Alan Cartridge (ink supplies)

2. Pulp Friction (juice bar)

1. The Yard (milkshake bar)*

---

* This would be even better if it was a boys-only milkshake bar, but apparently they're not willing to be sued for the sake of making a pun better. Cowards!

A list of what the platypus is called in different languages

5. Odd beak (Croatian)

4. Fat lips (Woiwurrung)

3. Broad nose (Icelandic)

2. Water mole (Arabic)

1. Duck mouth beast (Mandarin)

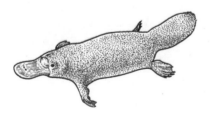

A list of international excuses

7. The bad workman blames his tools (English)

6. A bad wagoner blames the donkeys (Spanish)

5. If the farmer can't swim, it's due to his swimming trunks (German)

4. The skewed rocket is hindered by space (Bulgarian)

3. A heron blames the water because he cannot swim (Danish)

2. An ugly girl blames the mirror (Serbo-Croatian)

1. A poor dancer is impeded by his own balls (Russian)

A list of fun place names

8. Westward Ho! (Devon)

7. Kalamazoo (Michigan)

6. Knobhead (Antarctica)

5. Saint Louis-du-Ha!-Ha! (Québec)

4. Tickle Cock Bridge (Castleford)

3. Mianus (Connecticut)

2. Wigtwizzle (Peak District)

1. Cookie Town (Oklahoma)

A list of how to say 'Speak of the devil' in different countries

5. Speak of the donkey (Greece)

4. When you speak of the trolls, they stand in the entrance hall (Sweden)

3. Mention the lion, he eats you (Tunisia)

2. Remember the shit, here it is (Russia)

1. I wish I had said 'a million pounds' (Egypt)

A list of the number of words per language (roughly)

7. Taki Taki (340)

6. Classical Latin (40,000 – all boring)

5. Malay (83,000)

4. French (135,000)

3. German (330,000)

2. English (500,000)

1. Pedantese (Depends how you count hyphenated words. Or morphemes/lexemes. Either way you're probably wrong)

A list of books and the time it took to write them

8. Old Testament (1,000 years)

7. *The Catcher in the Rye* (10 years)

6. *Lord of the Flies* (5 years)

5. *1984* (1 year)

4. *Twilight* (3 months)

3. *A Clockwork Orange* (3 weeks)

2. *The Boy in the Striped Pyjamas* (2.5 days)

1. My first novel (I don't mean to brag … but watch out, Old Testament)

A list of excellent real florist names

7. Florist Gump

6. Austin Flowers

5. Back to the Fuchsia

4. The Lone Arranger

3. Judy's Garlands

2. Floral and Hardy

1. How Mad is She?

A list of titles of real research papers

5. Can a Cat Be Both a Solid and a Liquid? (physics)

4. The Effect of Country Music on Suicide (medicine)

3. Chickens Prefer Beautiful Humans (interdisciplinary)

2. Why Do Old Men Have Big Ears? (anatomy)

1. Salmonella Excretion in Joy-Riding Pigs (biology)

A bonus list of the single best title for a research paper ever

1. In March 2006 Professor Daniel M. Oppenheimer published a paper that argued writers seem more intelligent when using simple words than fancy ones. His paper was titled 'Consequences of Erudite Vernacular Utilized Irrespective of Necessity'*

---

* Oppenheimer should verily be extolled for his utilisation of brobdingnagian lexeme and magniloquent verbosity to manifest a humorously sesquipedalian appellation

A list of Russian expressions

7. That's no potato (that's no laughing matter)

6. Every barber knows that (it's a badly kept secret)

5. It's understandable to a hedgehog (it's simple)

4. Don't stir the tea with your penis (don't mess up)

3. Here's where the dog is buried (this is the crux of the issue)

2. Switch off the light and take out my suitcases! (OMG!)

1. Rope is good when it's long, speech is good when it's short (shut up now)

A list of medical treatments from the past

8. Vibrators (for female hysteria)

7. Cannibalism (for muscle cramps)

6. Heroin (for coughs)

5. Crystal meth (for asthma)

4. Arsenic (for arthritis)

3. Snail slime (for sore throats)

2. Blood of fallen gladiators (for epilepsy)

1. Teetotalism (to prevent spontaneous combustion)

A list of things that animals simply cannot do

7. Elephants (jump)

6. Crocodiles (move their tongues)

5. Rabbits (vomit)

4. Snow leopards (roar)

3. Lions (purr)

2. Birds (sweat)

1. Humans (keep New Year's resolutions)

A list of ten reasons why I didn't stick to my New Year's resolution

    1. Lazy

A list of words rarely seen without a prefix

8. Gruntled

7. Peccable

6. Advertently

5. Sensical

4. Couth

3. Trepid

2. Combobulated

1. Whelmed

A list of 'They lived happily ever after' in different languages

7. They lived well and we better (Greek)

6. They were happy and ate partridges (Spanish)

5. The tale is over and the aubergine is boiled (Tamil)

4. Snip, snap, snout, this tale's told out (Norwegian)

3. That was the length of it (Finnish)

2. And if they didn't die, they're still alive today (German)

1. Then along came a pig with a long nose and the story was over (Flemish)

A list of the five unwritten laws of concluding a book

    5.

    4.

    3.

    2.

    1.*

---

* These aren't necessarily in any order of importance

ABOUT THE AUTHOR

Adam is originally from Manchester but has moved around often (he's not very good at staying still). A list of some of the places where he's lived

8. London

7. Melbourne

6. Sydney

5. Queensland

4. The Channel Islands

3. The Canary Islands

2. Nashville

1. Newcastle upon Tyne

Adam has had over thirty jobs (he's not a very loyal employee either). A list of some of the things he's been paid to do

8. Teaching sport in kindergartens

7. Serving sandwiches in casinos

6. Catching footballs

5. Juggling bottles

4. Washing dishes

3. Reviewing music

2. Changing nappies

1. Walking on stilts

And here, in closing, is a list of Adam's proudest achievements to date

5. Year 8 table tennis champion

4. Once almost managed to fold a fitted sheet

3. Taught his granddad to use the internet

2. Going a whole week without saying 'that's what she said'

1. This book

You can find Adam on Twitter (and tell him all the things he got wrong in this book) at @AdamCSharp

ACKNOWLEDGEMENTS

A list of people I would like to thank

10. Clare Rees, for the idea for the title and all the advice

9. Northumbria University, for the generous grant to do my PhD with them

8. The JULA team, especially Milly, Donna, and Jo

7. Jenny Knight, my fellow pig phrase enthusiast

6. Everyone at Orion/Trapeze, especially Georgia Goodall, for being so patient, and Jamie Coleman, a great editor and an even better pet haikuist

5. Tobias Biberbach, for helping with my bad German, and Irina Sabatina, for helping with my really bad Russian

4. Maysie and Paul, for the kitchen feedback sessions

3. Kit de Waal, for all the encouragement, inspiration, and friendship

2. The wonderful people who've supported me on Twitter (you know who you are)

1. Claudia Fellinger, for inspiring many of the lists*

---

* This list is in no particular order because, obsessed as I am with everything being in order, ranking people I know is a step too far (just)

CREDITS

Trapeze would like to thank everyone at Orion who worked on the publication of *The Correct Order of Biscuits*.

AGENT
Jo Unwin

EDITOR
Jamie Coleman

COPY-EDITOR
Steve O'Gorman

PROOFREADER
Sally Sargeant

EDITORIAL MANAGEMENT
Georgia Goodall
Jane Hughes
Alice Davis
Claire Boyle

AUDIO
Paul Stark
Amber Bates

CONTRACTS
Anne Goddard
Paul Bulos
Jake Alderson

DESIGN
Lucie Stericker
Joanna Ridley
Nick May
Clare Sivell
Helen Ewing

FINANCE
Jennifer Muchan
Jasdip Nandra
Rabale Mustafa
Elizabeth Beaumont
Sue Baker
Tom Costello

MARKETING
Tanjiah Islam

PRODUCTION
Katie Horrocks
Fiona McIntosh

PUBLICITY
Patricia Deveer

SALES
Laura Fletcher
Victoria Laws
Esther Waters
Lucy Brem
Frances Doyle
Ben Goddard
Georgina Cutler
Jack Hallam
Ellie Kyrke-Smith
Inês Figuiera
Barbara Ronan
Andrew Hally
Dominic Smith
Deborah Deyong
Lauren Buck
Maggy Park
Linda McGregor
Sinead White
Jemimah James
Rachael Jones
Jack Dennison
Nigel Andrews

Ian Williamson
Julia Benson
Declan Kyle
Robert Mackenzie
Imogen Clarke
Megan Smith
Charlotte Clay
Rebecca Cobbold

OPERATIONS
Jo Jacobs
Sharon Willis
Lisa Pryde

RIGHTS
Susan Howe
Richard King
Krystyna Kujawinska
Jessica Purdue
Louise Henderson

Help us make the next generation of readers

We – both author and publisher – hope you enjoyed this book. We believe that you can become a reader at any time in your life but we'd love your help to give the next generation a head start.

Did you know that 9 per cent of children don't have a book of their own in their home, rising to 13 per cent in disadvantaged families*? We'd like to try to change that by asking you to consider the role you could play in helping to build readers of the future.

We'd love you to think of sharing, borrowing, reading, buying or talking about a book with a child in your life and spreading the love of reading. We want to make sure the next generation continue to have access to books, wherever they come from.

And if you would like to consider donating to charities that help fund literacy projects, find out more at **www.literacytrust.org.uk** and **www.booktrust.org.uk**.

THANK YOU

*As reported by the National Literacy Trust